MW00426621

STRANGE FIRE

Examining Motives in Ministry and Discerning the Offerings of the Heart

DR. MATTHEW STEVENSON

Table of Contents

Foreword by Apostle Greg Howse

Introduction

1   Motives: The Part That Matters Most

2   The Role and Nature of Discernment:
           Measuring by the Word

3   In Search of the AUTHENTIC: Exposing
           Fraudulence

4   Learning to be a "Heart Reader"

5   The Cynical Patterns of Flattery

6   Critical Connections and Pivotal Partnerships

Conclusion

Foreword

3 Who may ascend into the hill of the LORD? Or who may stand in His holy place? 4 He who has clean hands and a pure heart, Who has not lifted up his soul to an idol, Nor sworn deceitfully.

As we consistently, methodically move toward the dispensation of the fullness of times, there is increasing dialogue about accessing the presence of God, angelic visitations, and manifestations of glory. However, Psalm 24:3,4 provides three conditions for entering the supernatural realm. We must have clean hands. We must have a pure heart. And, we must be absolutely clear in our allegiance to the Most High God. "Clean hands" refers to our behavior, or lifestyle, especially where our relationships are concerned. "Pure heart" refers to functioning in life with pure motives.

In his new book, Strange Fire, Dr. Matthew Stevenson presents a case for living and ministering from a pure heart. A pure heart is characterized by pure motives. Dr. Stevenson writes, "We can no longer be content with existing within the confines of futile interactions that prove reckless, and in some cases fatal to destinies. We must actively pursue PURE motives. We must train those submitted to us to pursue PURE motives." As he continues in his narrative, Dr. Stevenson communicates his strong conviction concerning this issue of PURE motives.

The author provides an effective presentation of the need for keen discernment; and the danger of fraudulent ways in short-cutting our way to demonstrating the power of

God. Dr. Stevenson encourages the reader to discern personal motives in every aspect of life. He places strong emphasis on being authentic in life and ministry, as well as the required process to set a high standard of authenticity.

One of the Beatitudes presented in Matthew 5 is, "Blessed are the pure in heart, for they shall see God." This is the heart of Matthew Stevenson's writing. Another acceptable way of communicating this statement of Jesus is, "Blessed are those with pure motives, for they shall see as God sees." I know that as you read this book you will be encouraged to see yourself and see the world in which you live just as God sees it.

Greg Howse, Apostle
Cornerstone Christian Center
Sharpening Stone Group

Introduction

The heart, the scripture teaches, is the center and the seat of all human activity. Our interactions are determined by the state and the position of the heart. It is often very difficult to discern the position of the heart when one's actions have stemmed from that place for so long. For all of the transition and activity going on in our culture, ministry and the world, we are in need of a greater sensitivity to see what inspires us to do what we do. Every action we take in this hour should be measured by the standard of Jesus Christ and His word. Anything less than the absolute standards of the word of God will not do. We must become intolerant of everything attempting to take root in our lives that come from places in our hearts that have yet to submit to the work of the cross.

The scriptures are replete with examples of how the POSITION of the heart is important to God. We have come to learn over time that it's not what you do that pleases God; it's why you do what you do that glorifies Him most. This is a simple yet difficult truth to conceptualize because of the nature of the process that's presented once we realize we must measure our motives. For every action, word, decision and desire, there is a corresponding inspiration that comes from the heart. In modern Christianity, there is a tendency to place emphasis on that which is done externally without giving clear chance to judge the place of origin of those actions. This has caused great damage to innocent people over the past few decades who have been introduced to the vile and wicked nature of hearts even when the owner of the heart is considered 'Christian'.

It has been my personal experience that impure motives can be extremely damaging to the seasons and situations of God in your life. When God begins to orchestrate divine times in your life, encountering persons with demonic motivations can sabotage those purposes and potentially damage your interactions with future connections. In your pursuit of purpose, Satan works tirelessly to strategically place persons in your life and in your path that will cause you to become distracted and cause detriment to your future. If these motives are discerned before time, we will protect our focus, draw nearer to God and become the people that God has ordained that we be.....from the inside out.

As far as God is concerned, your life is a gradual processional leading up to the point of your maturity and readiness to conquer in your cause and succeed in your purpose. These are not the secret desires of your own heart, but the design of heaven for your very existence. With this powerful amount of pressure applied to your life, choices, actions, and connections comes a corresponding need to develop an acute awareness of the activity of your heart and the motivations behind your movement. In today's world of 'smoke and mirrors' Christianity, we are doing the world a disservice by representing our God erroneously through our failure to maturely discern our motives, correct our actions and repent when needed when our motives have caused detriment to someone's focus, perception of God, or Christian life.

In my estimation of things, I believe that every minister, leader and Christian should engage in a thorough study of the subject of heart motives and allow the axe of the word of God to descend mercilessly on the root of the issues. I believe if more ministers would dare take on such a journey, there would be less damage in the lives of innocent people at the hand of careless leaders. In over a decade of ministry experience, one of the most important skills I have learned to develop and am STILL learning to perfect is the ability to accurately perceive the motives and positions of hearts. May your journey to become as the son of God in the earth today be filled with an enriching experience that will teach you the importance of judging, weighing and knowing the truth of the matter.

Tirelessly Pursuing Christ-Likeness,
Dr. Matthew Stevenson

MOTIVES:
THE PART THAT MATTERS MOST

1

The words of Jesus spring loud and clear today: "If the Salt looses its savor, what is its purpose?" (Luke 14:34) These words in context address us as disciples in reference to our placement and purpose in a world ruled by darkness. Deeper into the text, we see other profound principles that we can apply toward our topic study of 'motives'. Jesus makes a point that every created thing has a purpose, and deep within that purpose we find the part that matters most. In anything that exists within the realm of creation, we find that there is a most important part. In this text, Jesus is highlighting the point or the purpose of salt and implies that the most important part is saltiness or savor. In life, ministry and relationships, there is a tendency to unconsciously neglect or ignore the part that matters most. If we look in this concept, we find that though created things are generally a collaboration of systems, parts and functions, there is still a part that matters most. If a stove cannot cook, it is useless; if a battery cannot energize, it is worthy of trash; if an iron cannot press, it should not be kept. In life, there is ALWAYS a part that matters most. Dare we look at our actions, choices, decisions or relationships in this same way? Many of us (especially in modern ministry) entertain peoples, places and things, overlooking the part that matters most. Ministry or service in any form unto God is not just a calling - it is also an offering. Though we have been destined or created to do whatever it is that we do, it is still an offering to a Holy God. Scripturally, God has never been under obligation to receive everything offered to him.

In Genesis 4: 1-5, we see the story of the seed of Adam, Cain and Abel. This is the first example of an offering being rejected by the Lord. Many of us make the very dangerous mistake of neglecting the fact that all we do FOR the Lord is primarily UNTO the Lord. This is in our ministries, our choices, our decisions and ultimately our destiny. When it comes to our offering, the position of the heart is what matters most. Just because something is 'Christian' in nature does not mean that it is always acceptable unto the Lord. Cain was doing a very 'Christian' thing by creating an offering to the Lord in the same manner as his brother, but God would not be fooled by his sanctimonious posture. His murderous heart position, filled with contempt and envy, spoke LOUDER to God than any prayer he offered during a religious ceremony. God, as always, weighed his heart. Prior to the time that the altar was built and effort was put into killing an offering, God saw the heart's position as distasteful; therefore, God REJECTED his offerings.

I believe that much of our more common ministry and relationship dealings, though 'Christian' looking, fall short of qualifying as pleasing to the Lord. In our offerings, our motives are what matter most. If the heart is to serve as an altar before the Lord, then this means our relationships, choices, actions and deeds are the offerings upon the altar. When impure, demonic or fleshly motivations are interbred with our offerings, then God rejects the contaminated offerings. The position of the heart is what really speaks to the Lordship of Jesus in our lives. If Christ is not the standard for how we interact with one another then we have been shortchanged in our experience with the Lord. Popular Christian speakers and even the organizations we accept as valid ministries are mostly nothing more than rejected offerings trying to masquerade their way into some sense of realness because of their blatant neglect of the part that matters the most - the reason WHY they do WHAT they do. God has never been and will never be deceived by the outer appearance of anything. No matter how well-polished, functional or excellent something may appear, God is always watching and craving for the part that matters most – motives. As we become more like Him, we should also be more unwilling to be ones that are content only with the appearance of something or another person's attempts to 'appear' like something. We must be equally skilled in discerning when we are substandard in our offerings and when another person is as well. This habit will cause us to continue to draw near to a Holy God who is more than deserving of Holy Offerings.

The flesh, if not restrained (or more appropriately) crucified, will attempt to get away with anything. It is ruthless. Far too many Christians underestimate how vile the flesh and heart is. This can become confusing to the unskilled or the novice discerner because many times fleshly actions, choices and relationships are dressed in Christian garb. The terms used can sometimes indicate a spirit-led or motivated movement/action. It is not until the fruit is examined and the heart is weighed that the truth of the matter is known. Unfortunately, we have all at some time or another been guilty of being one with an impure motive or being victimized by another who has impure motives. An awareness of this as a reality, as well as a willingness to submit this as our PRIMARY offering to the Lord (our motives) for His fire and dealings to consume is the only way to real power in these days and relationships that are worth keeping.

Treating our actions commonly when it comes to why we do what we do will cause us to fall prey to all sorts of deceptions and trickery from hell. Again, in any offering or interaction, what motivates us is the most important factor. Being human for the believer is no excuse to ignore the massively devastating role that impure motives can play in our decisions and interactions. The highest purposes of God for many lives have been frustrated and even compromised because a person who is fragmented never learned how to submit their motives and reasons to the Lord. This leaves you and I to be victim to a celebrity ministry market that impresses, blows away and fascinates us, but leaves us to fall short of God's intended purposes for cities and nations around the globe. We must do more than know that this is a possibility. We must examine ourselves and then learn to be trained to examine others. We can no longer be content with existing within the confines of futile human interactions that prove reckless and in some cases, fatal to destinies. We must actively pursue PURE motives. We must train those submitted to us to pursue PURE motives.

What matters most should always get the most attention. It is not wise to pay the most attention to things that matter the least. The position of the heart, or the inspiration behind actions, is what's weighed in the eyesight of God. One can imply from this fact that part of being Godly is also learning to perceive the part that matters most. If we do not learn to discern motives, whether good OR bad, we miss the richness of the vast experiences necessary to aide us in our growth. We must learn to invest effort in trying motives according to scriptures. This should be done if we intend to experience fullness. Man

Motives: The Part That Matters Most

looks on the OUTER appearance (1 Samuel 16:7). Our carnal nature is trained to be convinced by the outer. Most people have also learned to skillfully present the outward appearance to be deceitful. Most ministry markets or even basic Christian relationships are filled with people who have perfected the ability to convince people with the outer appearance. This is not just clothes and garb, but conversations, demeanors, expressions and religious scripts that fit the bill as acceptable to the undiscerning believer. From this, we deduce that a natural by-product of TRUE spirituality is the ability to see what is not seen. This principle is generally used in reference of faith, but we must also use it in the context of learning to become perceptive to the things that matter most - the activity and thoughts of the heart.

Our God is indeed a HOLY GOD. It is more than an attribute; it is who He is. The Bible is a complete eternal explanation of the holiness of God. Our heart is an instrument that was created to glorify God in its movements. We must be more cautious about what our hearts offer God. This is not just talking about praise and thanksgiving, but even more so, our dealings with others. Again, everything that we do in ministry or life that we consider is FOR the Lord should also be done as UNTO the Lord. This requires a greater consciousness about our dealings with others and our honesty with what transpires in our hearts on a day-to-day basis. These things determine what we do, what we say, what we project and what we hide from the light. Real biblical maturity is learning to pay attention to what matters most and learning to place less emphasis on what matters least to God..

THE ROLE AND NATURE OF DISCERNMENT: MEASURING BY THE WORD

2

"...And to some...Discerning of Spirits...." (1 Corinthians 12:10)

At present, we have seen a tremendous restoration of the gifts of the Spirit. The charismatic wave that hit America and the world in the mid 60's has now come to full popularity and there seems to be no place in the world where some form of spiritual gift is not regularly used. Even those who don't have a typical predisposition towards Pentecostal expression are also developing a new openness, in some degree or another, to the biblical administration of the gifts of the Spirit. There are still some evangelical groups that fight the biblical interpretation of the gifts but, for the most part, the charismatic release is on the rise! With this said, I have encountered thousands of people who have had knowledge of and flowed regularly in the gifts of the Spirit, but I believe the gift of discerning of spirits is the gift that is probably used the least in today's world. Typically, we interpret this gift or ability of the Holy Spirit to being the gift that allows us to sense or feel when something is not right about something. But there is much richer definition to this gift than what we have come to know. The gift of discerning of spirits is the ability to detect, by the Holy Spirit, motives and inspirations behind actions or events. The gift of discerning of spirits allows the believer to have revelation concerning the origin of an action or happening. It is so vital in these days to place priority in developing the gift of discerning of spirits. There are those in the world today who are immature and underdeveloped, but there are also those who are used by hell to cause detriment to the purposes of God for your life and ministry. Over the years, discernment can become dull. There is a need to sharpen discernment in every season. In many cases, there are external circumstances that can affect your level of discernment. We are living in days where perversion is prevalent and the enemy is now blurring the lines between the holy and the profane and is, even in some cases, developing theological support for perverse actions and hidden darkness. This is why it's important that we learn to routinely practice the ability of discerning spirits. I believe God wants all of his people to practice good discernment. A disciplined study life in the word of God will cause us to become sharp discerners. The Bible teaches us the following about the function of the word of God in our lives:

Hebrews 4:12 (Amplified): "For the Word that God speaks is alive and full of power [making it active, operative, energizing, and effective]; it is sharper than any two-edged sword, penetrating to the dividing line of the breath of life (soul) and [the immortal] spirit, and of joints and marrow [of the deepest parts of our nature], exposing and sifting and analyzing and judging the very thoughts and purposes of the heart."

The word of God judges. It is the highest authority on planet earth. Everything that God creates is founded upon the precedents of His word. We see very clearly in our verse that the word of God discerns the "deepest parts of our nature". Holding fast to our responsibility to study the word daily, we inherit an ability to detect motives. The trick is this - many of us seek to excel in our ability to detect the motives of others and, while this is very important, there are not always bad or negative things in the hearts of others. Many times we need to be able to discern good as well. In addition to learning to discern others, we must use this same gift of discernment to detect the movement and motivations of our OWN hearts. This is where maturity comes in. If we dedicate ourselves to paying attention to what's important to God, which we learned in the prior chapter is the posture of our hearts, then we are now challenged to practice discernment on our own hearts without personal bias! Is this possible? Absolutely! The word of God, when given absolute priority over our lives, thoughts and actions, serves no bias and supports no personal preferences – it only heralds ONE opinion and ONE view. When we make this view and this opinion our priority, believing even the hardest of its truths, we are then ready to embrace the full measure of the gift of discernment. We need discernment in our lives because we are trained to live according to the outer appearance. Unfortunately, the outer appearance does not have the strength to bridge us into our destinies and purposes. Many people will become and have already become quite famous by providing an outer appearance that guards the truth or reality of how sick and perverse the heart really is. Being emotionally drawn and attracted to such things are only the result of one thing - the lack of true biblical discernment. Going a step further, only a completely demonized individual will come to such a place of accurately discerning what's in their own heart and choosing to ignore it for fame, glamour or glitz. If we're lucky, they don't see it; if we are not as lucky, we live in a generation who chooses to neglect what they are shown by the word of God about their own hearts. What a crisis this is! Widespread is the great tragedy of self deception... those who refuse to examine, weigh, measure and discern not just others, but their own actions. This journey begins at very meager places. It begins by simply asking questions:

Why do I desire this?

Why do I want to do this?

What is inspiring me to speak with this one?

What is motivating me to be connected with or befriend this one?

These preliminary questions can lead you on a journey of answers that, if dealt with properly, can be judged by the word of God and can eventually become a new level of brokenness that God will never despise. Strange fire is the offering of the heart that does not meet the requirements of the word. Our friendships, conversations, choices, and daily actions are to be done as unto the Lord. If our lives are to bring total glory to Him as Lord, then everything we do should be pleasing to Him. How we treat everything we're involved in should be pleasing to Him. The motives of our hearts should glorify the Lord and not shame His intentions for our lives. The gifts of the Spirit are meant to glorify the Lord and bring the highest potential out of the believer. The gift of discerning of spirits is meant to protect us and our relationships from demonic sabotage because of unseen motives in us or others. Discernment can only be cultivated by an honest and transparent relationship with the scriptures, allowing it to detect, sever and judge the actions of our lives. There are other functions to the gift of discerning of spirits, but I will only focus on this one function for the purpose of our study. Oftentimes we can 'feel' when our motives are not Godly or come from soulish origins – even if we are not honest with others about it. The gift of discernment helps us to see wrong motives with clarity and acknowledge its presence in our hearts. Without acknowledgement of its presence in our hearts, it is impossible to come into repentance. For a walk of intimacy with the Lord that is full of zeal and passion, we must sift through our daily actions and involvements with others through the fire of the word of God so that our daily offerings (life choices and decisions) are pleasing to him. The word of God has the power through the illumination of the Holy Spirit to give us greater articulation to what's going on inside our hearts. The determining factors to our movements can only be tracked by the powerful presence of the word of God. A person who has no desire to be closer to the Lord will employ none of these instructions. Such people are content with doing just enough to appear to be healthy, stable or honest before the eyes of men. Those who desire to purge their lives of any strange offerings realize the importance of allowing the penetrating power of the word of God to make our actions and inspirations just as holy as our confessions. The gift of discerning of spirits is key in this matter. We need the instructions of the Holy Spirit in identifying motivating factors. Without discipline in discernment, we run the risk of breeding a lawless generation of 'Christians' who deal ruthlessly with one another because of a heart that has not learned obedience to the ways of God. The word of God provides the sole power to determine how an action should be judged. It is by the spirit that we are quickened to this fact and empowered to overcome it by repentance and confession. If leaders would be more proactive about this in private quarters, there would be way less scandal before public sight.

IN SEARCH OF THE AUTHENTIC: EXPOSING FRAUDULENCE

3

In today's world, expedience is the order of the day. The worldwide web, fast food industry and even computer technology display the lack of patience in modern society. Though in many ways our convenience is important in being able to accomplish quickly, it should never be at the cost of sacrificing quality or authenticity. In addition to being extremely fast-paced, we are also less interested in paying costs for things that can be gotten cheaper. From a sales perspective, this is not such a bad thing, but from the Kingdom's point of view, anything worth having and presenting to the world should be extremely costly. The value of what we present to the world should be high and capable of breaking bondages. If we settle for a "cheap" expression of ministry, relationships and service, we will allow Satan a right to advance his propaganda throughout generations. In any urban city you will find access to 'bootleg' films and pseudo clothes that are good imitations of the real name brand. These trends are not different in any way from things that are happening in the realm of the spirit. We have raised a generation afraid to pay the price of fasting, prayer, study, honesty and humility to have genuine experiences with God and with people that lead us into world change. The Spirit of the Lord began to speak very clearly to me concerning His desire to deal with the 'spirit of fraudulence'.

This is not a light thing. If God is to be glorified above the Kingdoms of the world, we must be willing to invest whatever it takes to hold, handle and move in authentic power and authority. Our authority, power and destiny cannot be solely based on talent, name-dropping or impressive marketing and media. It must be developed through paying the high price of judging the heart and presenting motives before the Lord. The spirit of fraudulence is a demonic force that easily entices men and women to take quick routes in their walks with the Lord and developmental relationships to quickly arrive to points of fame and popularity. This is where our motives come in. When a journey looks too complicated or requires too much effort from the person who is un-whole, it is the easy or cheap thing to do to settle for the first door that looks like the ticket to arrival.

There is ALWAYS danger in resurrection without a cross. This is not speaking of the cross of persecution and testing, but the self-inflicting sacrifice of committing to purity, wholeness and refusal to resemble darkness on any level. This is a process, and God will allow you to experience portions of who you are called to be while you are in the process, but it's a crisis when you settle at this place. Many Christian leaders have settled at a place where they are now in denial about their motives and 'Christianize' them with spiritual terminology, only to be continually devastated when the Love of God restrains them to the level they are REALLY ready to handle. This scenario can often feel like punishment or even being teased, but it is really the grace of God at work in the life of the fledgling.

"They'll see," or "I'll show them someday," is the all too common cry of the leader scurrying to find their place of significance and validity on the ministry or world front. With this seed of revenge aimed at whoever the audience may be (this will vary based upon life experience), the individual finds him or herself conjuring up a power, authority, wisdom and a confidence that does not really exist. The trick is that the talent this person possesses is enough to get them open doors to be heard. Our challenge, though, is not whether or not their voice should be heard; it's whether or not it should be heard while the MOTIVES of the individual have not been surrendered to the dealings of the Lord. We must lose the need to be impressive in this hour! The authentic, and the process that it requires to be authentic, as well as the price that it takes to remain authentic, requires details that the fraudulent are not interested in. Ministry circles who are eagerly excited to get into social settings where they endlessly meander down conversational roads about names, suits, numbers, amounts and other things that don't resemble the heart and nature of genuine biblical relationships. It is my greatest dread that this generation has become so accustomed and infatuated with what is fake that they have been trained to reject the true. Many "spiritual fathers" of the old order (old is not in reference to age but season) really resemble managers of the budding R&B singer or potential NBA star, looking for the newest undiscovered talent that can bring another realm of influence to themselves. Real fatherly ministry will result in sons and daughters who will not relent until they have become authentic.

We must acknowledge that the flesh (the nature, system and tendencies of humanity without an experience with Jesus) will get away with whatever it can get away with. Having to submit to the Cross is something it doesn't and won't ever desire to do. This is a known fact, but it is not a truth that most individuals like to meditate upon when studying the topic of motives. We must crucify the flesh. Masquerade ministry pursuits will only allow you space to restrain it, but the Apostle Paul encourages us to KILL IT! (Galatians 5:24) The flesh is the culprit behind why impure motives are left for years unchecked. A desire to 'get even' with crowds that abused you, overlooked you or refused to believe in your purpose places a carnal drive in you that allows deep seated evils to hide themselves in your heart. These are motives that exist in people and the primary reason for many of today's scandal. Learn to aggressively deal with the temptation of the flesh to bring you into fraudulence.

Lets examine the term 'fraudulent':

A deception deliberately practiced in order to secure unfair or unlawful gain. One who assumes a false pose; an impostor; deliberate deception, trickery, or cheating intended to gain an advantage. (Farlex Free Dictionary)

The AUTHENTIC ministry, message and genuine motives of a well-trained minister will released unprecedented change and results in the lives of all who encounter him. The fraudulent will only do enough to lead people back to him for self-gratifying purposes. The majority of fraudulent activity is characterized by being impressive. This is not to say that there are genuine people who cannot be impressive, but this is one of the tell-tale signs of those whose motives reek of demonic influence. People generally labor and work effortlessly to become impressive to cover the motives behind their actions and movement. Our culture thrives on the impressive, which is why the entertainment industry is so massively pulsating with wealth. People desire to be impressed. The problem with this is the Kingdom has no use for those that simply desire to be impressive. The Kingdom has use for those who are committed to becoming as genuine and sincere as the son of God was. Deceit, trickery, dishonesty are clear traits in the heart language of those that are fearful of enduring a process that brings judgment upon the motives of the heart. *their own*

It is not until the Church realizes that our works are still not what pleases the Lord. It seems that we understand the 'works' mentality when attempting to understand the message of Grace, but we seem to leave it there. The scriptures say that we are to repent of DEAD works. (Hebrews 6:1-3) I believe a dead work is any work or effort that comes from a place rooted in your ways. We must realize that if we do great works for God, but we refuse to allow Him to deal with our ways, our *yessss!* works have no real foundation! Our "ways" if not dealt with can become a detriment to the works that God has called us to build. It doesn't matter how many contacts we have, invitations we get, numbers that attend or nations we visit. If our ways bring no glory to God, then it is impossible for our works to do so. We are not without exciting resumes of works that speak loud and clear (or so it seems) to our standing in heaven and our endorsement of the Father, but what we are without is a generation in passionate pursuit of the WAYS of God. At times, God will even allow people to hear His voice and release it to others through preaching, teaching, prophecy, etc. We know from scripture any (created) THING can hear his voice. Balaam's ass is a clear example of this prophetic phenomenon, noted in Numbers 22:1-35. It takes relationship, communion and commitment to know the WAYS of God. The capability of hearing God's voice is not restricted even from the sinner. God speaking to you requires no relationship or communion. God always spoke to objects in scripture. However, knowing his WAYS requires a commitment, a consciousness and a communion deeper than what most people are willing to invest in. *fear of the Lord! Ps. 25:14*

Strange Fire

Favor comes to people who change their ways!

Proverbs 16:7 – "When a man's WAYS are pleasing to the Lord, God makes even his enemies to be at peace with him."

If we are to gain access into portions of our culture that hate our God and make a mockery of His Christ, we must pursue the kind of walks and relationships that allow our WAYS or MOTIVES to be pleasing to the Lord. God will cause even our enemies to open doors of access to us when we please Him because He is certain that we won't switch our allegiance.

1. The first step towards being authentic is the acknowledgement of the tendencies alive in your heart that lead to being fake. There are those alive in the earth today that are desperately seeking the TRUE AND LIVING GOD!!! They have not been able to find answers in the guy who people preach about on TVs or the one people sing about on radios. I believe this is because of the massive breach between our works and our ways. These people are searching for the Lord GOD of Elijah: the one who has never lost a battle; the one who triumphs over all of his enemies; the one whose great exploits serve as a monument to generations to come. They are looking for a REAL God. The chaos and hopeless environment that the absence of the true church has caused in the world has also stirred such a depravation and hunger as we have never seen before. This hunger is provoking the Mighty One. HE IS NOT GOING TO STAY SILENT. God is moving now and will continue to move in mammoth measures. It is up to us to be authentic vessels that He can use to display his magnitude and greatness in the face of the heathen.

Are you guilty of fraud? Have you lived a life or attempting to make a connection for the wrong reasons? Have you spent your energy trying to become something that satisfies the needs or perceptions of men while avoiding the requirements of heaven for your life?

There are many fashionable religious trends that are now sweeping American Christianity. Many of them are cheap attempts at restoring biblical principles, but of course, without the cost of pure motives. These trends are expressions of the strange fire bellowing out from the hearts of men and women who love ministry more than Him. One of the more dangerous trends is the "Spiritual Father-Spiritual Son" paradigm. God has been visiting the issue of the spiritual fathers after the manner of the Apostle Paul perhaps over the last few decades. There has come a recent trend where everyone is beginning to embrace this role beyond the process of the judging of motives. This is also true with 'covering' agreements and arrangements. This is a subject special to my heart because God calls apostolic fathers to protect the universal church. This is not a book on this subject, but it bears the necessity that I address the crisis involved with these happenings. We need authentic measuring lines for such relationships. The devil is out to pervert this concept to frustrate the purposes of God for successive generations. The illegitimate manner in which these relationships 'occur' prove how fraudulent they are. In many cases, there is no time invested, no insight into the personal lives or involvements of the son, and no real sense of responsibility for the actions of the son. These are only three areas that are very simple and yet speak to the very obvious reasons of the fraudulence in these relationships. Men who are estranged from the heart of the Father and the concern for sons that are genuine and authentic are now adopting the title of father without the heart posture to do so. This is mainly because of impure and (unhealed) motives. Fraud fathers are talent scouts and number hogs who never invest in the quality of the relationship with sons. Neither do they care about what heaven really cares about in the life of the sons. Many of them don't even have this very preliminary insight. In a spiritually orphaned world, many potential sons are gravitating to (anything) that will accept and affirm them as sons, and in most cases, they are ignorant to the biblical profile and heart posture of such a person. To them, any attention is better than no attention. There is only one cure for this: AUTHENTIC FATHERS must establish authentic relationships with sons and commit to building their lives from the inside out by being an advocate for what God is an advocate of in their lives.

When you examine the authentic next to the fraudulent, there is no comparison. This is true with relationships, personalities, products, etc. In our world, there are so few people who have made the commitment to being (authentic) that we are accustomed to the fraudulent. Being authentic requires a serious investment and will even make you go through seasons of being unpopular, but doing the (right) thing the (wrong) way is still doing the wrong thing! We are in need of genuine power, not smoke and mirrors. We are in need of real ministry, not just pulpit preaching. We are in need of authentic relationships, not just superficial associations for access into certain ministerial doors. May the Holy Spirit release his fire upon the issue of fraudulence and cause unrest in the heart of every reader until they come into the place of the authentic. When your life, motives and actions are authentic, your offerings are pleasing to the Lord. It is not until you know the fire of God that you can recognize that which is strange fire to Him! God, raise a generation who craves the authentic and expose the fraudulent!!

LEARNING TO BE A
"HEART READER"

4

John 3:1-9, Matthew 23:33

"You SNAKES, You brood of Vipers"

The purpose of this book is not to make anyone paranoid or critical of others. Its sole purpose is to heighten awareness regarding the need to sharpen discerning skills that help us to see when our motives go away from the standards of God, specifically as it pertains to ministry. This book or the revelations in it are not license to become skeptical for everyone that comes in your life. If anything, it's meant to shed light on your heart to help *help* prevent you from becoming a predator with impure motives. *me.*

Jesus and John the Baptist developed a critical ability during their ministry on earth. I believe because of the crucial nature of their assignments they would have to learn to be 'Heart Readers'. This means they both had to understand that out of value for the amount of time they were allotted by God for the completion of their task, they would have to learn to discern the hearts of men. When you know how time-sensitive your purpose and destiny is, you lose the desire to waste time by occupying your space with persons who are not connected to you and add no value to your life. The enemy is always out to devour time. Many of us make the mistake of allowing time to be invested in relationships that are not components that are important to our destiny. Had Jesus and John the Baptist overlooked this principle, focus would've been difficult for them to achieve. In the pursuit of destiny, focus is essential and distraction is deadly. This book is written mainly for preventive measures. It is not a scoffing tool to capitalize on the thousands of wrongly motivated leaders on the scene today, but to instruct us on how not to become what we've seen. Jesus was not willing to hand His destiny or the time given Him to complete it over to a group of poisonous snakes. He refers to them as snakes because of the cruel intentions and positions of their heart towards Him and the purposes of God. Being a heart reader requires an intentional development of the skill of discerning and detecting. We must learn to detect those that God sends to us and those that gravitate towards us for evil gain.

"The heart is deceitful above all things and desperately wicked! Who can know it?" Jeremiah 17:9 (KJV)

When it comes to your life, your reason for existing should be a primary focus for you. Having said this, you must learn to be well trained at perceiving the hearts of men towards you. This will help you to honor those that the Holy Spirit orchestrates for your improvement and also judge those that hell sends for your detriment.

Because the heart is deceitful or expert in dishonesty, we must learn how to read the heart through the pure lens of Christ-likeness. The more you are unlike Christ, the more impossible it is for you to become a viable source of judgment when it comes to reading hearts. Knowing intentions and motives requires seeing them as Christ sees them – Christ being the standard for what we 'see'. This is not a natural seeing with the natural eye, but it is more like an intentional detecting that will protect your assignment. Jesus routinely perceived the intentions of those around him. It was nothing for him to call out a crowd's thoughts, not from his prophetic office, but rather from his trained skill at perceiving hearts. (Matthew 9:4, 12:25)

How do we judge and measure hearts without human bias? How are we to learn to trust the signs that we detect from the hearts of men? How can we be sure that we 'see' what we really see? "

God, he is the one who knows everyone's heart..." Acts 15:8

Again, God is just. He is never biased. He is not convinced by flesh, neither is he moved by skepticisms. Knowing this, our only reliant source in accurately perceiving the hearts of men is becoming like him. If we are tolerant of anti-Christ traits in our lives, we should never trust ANYTHING we see about anyone's heart because it is seen through a lens unchanged. The only guarantee that you have perceived the intentions or heart of another is only found by your relentless pursuit of Godliness and Christ-likeness. Those who are honestly like God easily recognize those who are not. This requires uncanny honesty. Whatever you are prone to harbor in your life that is strange fire to God will hinder your ability to read the hearts of another.

"SEARCH ME, OH GOD, AND KNOW MY HEART: TRY ME AND KNOW MY THOUGHTS," (Psalms 139:23)

The first cry of anyone desiring to know the hearts of men and to detect the posture of hearts towards them is to cry like David did in Psalms 139:23.

Learning to be a "Heart Reader"

SEARCH ME, OH GOD - God is wise and omniscient. There really isn't a need for Him to search anything because nothing catches Him by surprise. He beholds both the end and the beginning. So the investigation is for us. It's a journey of the gradual exposure of things in the heart because of life experience that may conceal traits that are offensive to God.

TRY ME - This is the servant/sonship heart of David, giving God permission to place his desires to the test of time and attack. This measures the desperation level of the cry. Does your desire to stay pure remain intact even in unpleasant situations or seasons of attack? This is asking the Lord to show you the sturdiness of your cry for purity before Him and others.

KNOW MY THOUGHTS - This is the heart that God will not despise. The foremost cry of brokenness and the epitome of the contrite is asking God to confront your denial by being the final judge of your actions, desires, options, and motives.

This will be an intense journey, but nonetheless needed if you are to become MATURE. The cry of this book is for maturity. We must be willing to allow the Holy Spirit, who is our Teacher, to make us mature. There is no maturity greater than Christ-likeness. When the cry of your heart is to be like Christ, you can't help but SEE like Christ. Maturity is being able to discern the position of one's heart without developing a corresponding fleshly opinion about it. Making the necessary adjustments are one thing, but then responding in offense or even with an opinion is still unreflective of the Christ nature. We must learn to discern and not be personally affected to the point of sin for what we discern, even in peoples' hearts toward us.

"The (lamp of the) LORD's light penetrates the human spirit, exposing every hidden motive." Proverbs 20:27 (New Living Translation)

In perhaps the most powerful scriptural discourse of the significance of the word of God in our lives, Psalms 119, David gives us a pattern for the Lamp of the Lord. "THY WORD is a LAMP unto my feet and a light for my path." (Psalms 119:105)

This scripture unveils several keys to our pursuit of being accurate discerners of the heart. Cynicism and paranoia must be dealt with by the word of God if we are to ever mature to have healthy progressive involvement with others for the sake of our purpose. David describes the word of God as a lamp to our feet. Feet, in this sense, speaks to our movement and our motives. It speaks to our will and our desire. The word of God sheds its light on our movements, motives, will and desires. The light of this very same light (THE WORD) sheds illumination on our path which is otherwise in darkness. This darkness is our decisions, our choices and options. The word of God breaks the powers of darkness over our decisions, choices and options when it comes to our dealings with others.

Repeating at this point an already mentioned point, the word of God is the only key to excelling in any accurate discernment. One who is ignorant of the word of God will also be equally as blind to what's wicked in their hearts and can only assume what's wicked in the heart of another. This leads many people into tangled webs of involvement and association that are like cancer to the call of God on their lives. We need the word of God right and priority through daily devotion to allow it to expose every hidden motive. Not just others, but ours as well. This will allow us to be protective over the time we've been given and will also keep us Godly in the way the Lord desires. A daily study life will allow you to filter through the attributes and activities of your heart that are unpleasing to the Lord including your motives and inspirations. Many people have high aspirations to become great things, but their investigation practices of themselves and others are too low to allow them to be there.

Here is perhaps the most vital point in this section of the book. In learning to be a heart reader, you cannot ignore the powerful role of forgiveness; not superficial or fictitious forgiveness, but the real breaking of the heart and release of God's mercy and grace towards others. Without forgiveness, you are unable to see clearly. The hearts of any person will appear dark or demonically motivated if you still nurture unforgiveness toward any person, group of people or ministry that may have caused you harm. This is important. In this process, a real journey of forgiveness is absolutely essential to sharpening your discernment. When a person has been wounded, they learn to become skilled at recognizing the source or what appears to be the source of that wound even in the hands of new people or groups. The problem with this is, it may or not be the same scenario. Without a process of testing and weighing with the absolute authority being that of the light of God, you are only making an assumption from the place of past harm. Hurt, when left undealt with, will blind you from recognizing new enemies as well as hinder you from benefiting from the fruit of new covenant relationships. It's not comfortable, but it's a must. Unforgiveness blinds you, and your adversary would have it no other way. As long as you remain crippled in your ability to perceive accurately because of previous wounds you will always live, move and relate from an external place and die from internal bleeding.

Are you listening children?

Strange Fire

As you are crying for God to make you a heart reader, so that you can see from afar off, those that will be used by hell to take you off course, the only appropriate way to begin is to ask God to search YOU! Without this, you are nothing more than a demonized detective, rejecting the truth of the lamp of God searching through lens of hypocrisy for the error and poison in the hearts of those who seem to be against you.

Learning to be a "Heart Reader"

THE CYNICAL PATTERNS
OF FLATTERY

5

"These people honor me with their lips, but their hearts are far from me." Matthew 15:8 (NIV)

Flattery is a common sin amongst most modern ministry circuits. It's perhaps one of the cruelest tactics of Satan to prevent perception of his tactics through men with evil intentions. Flattery is the vocalization of praise, honor, commitment and approval beyond the corresponding relationship with the heart. People can speak beyond where their hearts are, or they can speak and cover up the true position of their heart.

Flattery is a disguise for an assassination attempt on your life. This does not qualify every compliment or positive statement of affirmation as a sign that something wicked is going to transpire. Flattery is the unreasonable, regular statement of high praise beyond a person's personal interactions with you. Oftentimes, people will do and say good things about you publicly and will not indicate that they feel the same way about you in private quarters. This is the sign of something demonic brewing. When Satan is planning a devastating emotional attack on you, he baits you through flattery. It is important that you pursue wholeness because, in some cases, flattery causes people to be exposed to abusive situations. Not only that, but to the one with low self esteem, flattery is the glue that keeps them in the abusive situation. With flattery also comes bribes. This may or may not be financial bribe. When people move in flattery, they are also common for testing what you will compromise to be seen in a certain light. Jesus experienced painful occasions with flattery. Whether it was the historic Judas kiss or the triumphal entry where people sang hosanna, only to turn around a few days later and cry, "Crucify him!", flattery is one of the ways the heart tells on itself. In ministry, people will boast of your abilities, giftedness, future or skill beyond their relationship or, in some cases, knowledge of you. This does well for promotional material and marketing. Satan is proud. When he is involved in anything he won't always keep quiet and go unseen. The scriptures give several warnings against those who do lip service that strokes ego and persona.

Isaiah 29:13 says, "Wherefore the Lord said, Forasmuch as this people draw near [me] with their mouth, and with their lips do honour me, but have removed their heart far from me, and their fear toward me is taught by the precept of men."

In this prophetic word, God says through the prophet Isaiah that the people guilty of flattery had only learned how to speak of him because they were taught a script by men. There are those today who are scripted in what they say to you and over you. They know lingo that is good enough to hook you in to believing something that you shouldn't believe. I have also seen cases where flattery was used to hinder your ability to perceive darkness in the person's life or intention towards you.

Let's examine more scriptures regarding flattery:

Flattery is a covenant breaking spirit. Those who use flattery are often used to sabotage your desire for genuine covenant.

Proverbs 2:16 – "to deliver you from the strange woman, from the adulteress who flatters with her words…"

Flattery is seductive and sweet to the hearing of those who hear it. Be careful not to allow her powers to destroy your future.

Proverbs 5:3 – "For the lips of a strange woman drop [as] an honeycomb, and her mouth [is] smoother than oil."

An addiction or acceptance of flattery exposes you to the powers of a curse.

Proverbs 22:14 – "The mouth of an adulteress is a deep pit; He who is cursed of the LORD will fall into it."

<u>Bible Verse Index on Flattery</u>

Saints should not use – Job 32:21-22

Ministers should not use – 1 Thessalonians 2:5

The wicked use, to…

Others – Psalm 5:9; 12:2

Themselves – Psalm 36:2

Hypocrites use, to God – Psalm 78:36

Those in authority – Daniel 11:34

The Cynical Patterns of Flattery

False prophets and teachers use – Ezekiel 12:24; Romans 16:18

Wisdom, a preservative against – Proverbs 4:5

Worldly advantage obtained by – Daniel 11:21,22

Seldom gains respect – Proverbs 28:23

Avoid those given to – Proverbs 20:19

Danger of – Proverbs 7:21-23; 20:5

Punishment of - Job 17:5; Psalm 12:3

CRITICAL CONNECTIONS AND PIVOTAL PARTNERSHIPS

6

The Book of Genesis is the book of beginnings. If we are to be the PEOPLE of God, we must rely on the word of God as the sole standard for how we build every aspect of our lives. We must learn how to embrace relationships so that we don't abort the purposes of God and frustrate the mandate of heaven on our lives. Many Christians subconsciously sabotage right relationships to either keep demonic ones, or to maintain a posture or lifestyle that is not pleasing to God.

Relationships are the provision of God for mankind to prosper us, to bless us and to usher us into our destinies. Many Christians tragically rely on worldly concepts for building and measuring relationships and are disappointed to find out that they lead to repetitive cycles. Many Christians rely on worldly philosophies and ideologies to build relationships on. One relationship myth is that trust is the "foundation" for relationships. This is not true. Trust is one of the most important powers that drive a relationship but it is not the foundation. The foundation of every relationship should be the word of God, and the definition of God. Trust will grow. But trust is an insufficient foundation because the FLESH cannot be trusted.

Genesis 2:18 states, "It is not good for man to be alone." When

God determines that something is not good, we can only benefit by believing what he has determined. Relationships are under attack by hell, because it is through relationships that the purposes of God are advanced.

Many people look at Genesis 2:18 as a scripture for marriage, but we need to examine these scriptures in the light of relationships period. There are different kinds of relationships and different levels of relationships but ALL relationships/ associations need to be connected to purpose.

In the book of Genesis we see a pattern that God establishes an intimacy, an acquaintance, and WALK, with Adam before he adds the component of human relationship to his life. This reveals a profound truth about the way we are to approach relationships and divine connections.

There is a connection between Worship and Relationships. Churches with strong worship will have strong relationships. Worshippers are persons who are trusted of God and sought out of God. They are selfless, sacrificing and great confidants. The foundation of any connection should be strong worship and commitment to intimacy with God.

Paul admonishes in 2 Corinthians 6:14, "Be not unequally yoked..." That means not to be connected to or in covenant with those that are not burdened for Christ in the same way as you are or would like to be.

Never befriend the disobedient, the lawless or the rebellious. Their self worship will eventually become violent towards you and cause much grief.

God has established that worship be the breeding ground for destiny connections. According to John 4:23, God seeks worshippers; we should make it a habit to seek them as well. In order to build a habitation of God and a strong tabernacle for him to dwell, we must become intense worshippers, but as with any trait that belongs to humans, it is universal. If we learn to minister to the Lord, we will learn to minister to others.

Creating an environment of worship will ensure that God is the center for all of our interactions as people in the Kingdom. We must re-orientate ourselves regarding the relationships we have been blessed with and be open to improving them and placing honor upon them.

Relationships will either add to you or rob from you! There is no middle ground. Worshippers understand the importance of adding to. They never desire to rob!

Honor

We live in a world/society that does not emphasize the importance or significance of "honor". There has, throughout generations, been a gradual decline in the subject of honor. In the Kingdom, if we are to live by the laws of God, we must prioritize Honor as a part of our lives. There has been dishonor in our music. Dishonor in our language, Dishonor in our culture, Dishonor in our perspectives.

If anything is to grow, to be cultivated, or to be nurtured it can only be done by honor (e.g. Honor the Lord with the Substance) Psalms 19:14. Honor is the only way to multiply or to extend anything.

What is honor?
Honor is esteem, praise, to place value upon, to regularly (as a part of your custom) vocalize importance. Honor is an investment to multiply!!

When any relationship is deprived, it has been dishonored. Many people have relationships that stagnate and thereby lose purpose. Relationships are meant to be improved, cultivated and made better over the years; this can only be done through honor.

What does honor require?
RIGHT PERSPECTIVE – Perspective is what places relationship in proper place.
HUMILITY – One must humble oneself before they can place honor on another.
ACTION – Honor is a seed that must be SOWN. Without it, all connections will stagnate and die.

Honor, THAT YOUR DAYS MAY BE LONG is a command of God when referring to or engaging with sources of life. – When God wants to extend something, an area or someone, he demands that they live in a culture of honor.

In the KINGDOM, honor is regular. The lack of honor is a sign of carnality, pride, and resistance to the purposes of God.

Leaders must be honored with DOUBLE HONOR. Consider the teacher's pet. Why does everyone despise the teachers pet? Because everyone else is mediocre, the teacher's pet has learned an invaluable lesson: what you honor will bring you to promotion. What you honor will cause you to excel. The teacher's pet has learned to vocalize the value they see in who has the key to their future.

The Conflict of Honor and Expectation – Many people EXPECT beyond what they honor. Self-entitlement will destroy even God ordained relationships. You can only expect to the degree that you have honored.

Honesty and Transparency

There are three parties involved in every relationship: two people and the spirit driving the relationship (Eccl 4:12). If a demon or dark motivation is the driving force behind a relationship, then an individual will lack the ability to be completely honest or transparent because the Holy Spirit is the spirit of truth. God wants all our God ordained relationships to be healthy, living, getting better and glorifying him.

We have been learning vertical and horizontal relationship methods. These relationships are essential and must be discerned, developed and defended. Humans need healthy commitments. Without healthy commitments, there is no system of development active in the life of believers.

Honesty and transparency must be cultivated if we are to grow Godly relationships that are connected to the fulfillment of purpose. They reinforce the covenant and strengthen Godly bonds!

Honesty is more than telling the truth; it is the complete opening and tying of the heart. The byproduct of this is the details of our lives are exposed for the purpose of building us up in a Godly direction. Something motivated by demons cannot do this.

Ruth and Naomi's relationship display a large level of commitment; Ruth 1:16- Paul instructs us to be committed and transparent as 1. 1 Corinthians 1:10

Issues:
We are taught to façade. We are taught that vulnerability is a bad thing. We are motivated by fear to not be and ironically enough we feel safe that way.

Clear communication is honest and transparent and its driving force is a Godly commitment.

Transparency is living your life as an open book before those you are committed to and those that are committed to you. There is no other kind of truth other than the complete truth.

ASK YOURSELF THIS: WHAT IS THE REAL VALUE OF A RELATIONSHIP OR CONNECTION THAT I CANNOT BE TRANSPARENT WITH?

Honesty and transparency is an act of the will. Hiding and being deceitful can also be an act of the will.

What are the benefits of transparency? Your secrets will make you sick. Transparency will heal you.

Dishonesty breaks the hedges – "Whoso breaketh a hedge (honesty, counsel, safety) the serpent will bite." Ecclesiastes 10:8b

"Confess your faults, that you may be HEALED." James 5:16

(Things to Consider)
Who are the people in my life that I'm committed to and why?

Do these commitments glorify God, improve me or complete my destiny?
Am I completely honest/transparent with the people that I intend to be committed to?
Have I verbalized my commitments and my desire to be completely honest and transparent?
Do my commitments need to be reprioritized?

Genesis 11:6-9 (KJV) "And the LORD said, Behold, the people is one, and they have all one language; and this they begin to do: and now nothing will be restrained from them, which they have imagined to do. Go to, let us go down, and there confound their language, that they may not understand one another's speech. So the LORD scattered them abroad from thence upon the face of all the earth: and they left off to build the city. Therefore is the name of it called Babel; because the LORD did there confound the language of all the earth: and from thence did the LORD scatter them abroad upon the face of all the earth."

General Principles on Connections and Right Relationships
Communication a Heart Issue – "Out of the abundance of the heart the mouth speaks," Matthew 12:34b

People speak the language of their life – Whatever life has done to them determines how they communicate

Understanding how to communicate with those responsible for your growth and development

Building TOWER RELATIONSHIPS (relationships that affect generations) Learning to communicate is expensive (Who sets out to build a tower and doesn't count the cost)

Answer!

Proper Communicates Cancels Unnecessary Conflicts (Some conflict/confrontation needed and can be anointed)

1 Corinthians 1:10 – An Apostolic Call for UNITY through healthy communication
Transparency, Honesty, Consistency

1 Corinthians 1:7-12 (Amplified Bible)
"That you are not [consciously] falling behind or lacking in any special spiritual endowment or Christian grace [[a]the reception of which is due to the power of divine grace operating in your souls by the Holy Spirit], while you wait and watch [constantly living in hope] for the coming of our Lord Jesus Christ and [His] being made visible to all. And He will establish you to the end [keep you steadfast, give you strength, and guarantee your vindication; He will be your warrant against all accusation or indictment so that you will be] guiltless and irreproachable in the day of our Lord Jesus Christ (the Messiah). God is faithful (reliable, trustworthy, and therefore ever true to His promise, and He can be depended on); by Him you were called into companionship and participation with His Son, Jesus Christ our Lord. But I urge and entreat you, brethren, by the name of our Lord Jesus Christ, that all of you be in perfect harmony and full agreement in what you say, and that there be no dissensions or factions or divisions among you, but that you be perfectly united in your common understanding and in your opinions and judgments. For it has been made clear to me, my brethren, by those of Chloe's household, that there are contentions and wrangling and factions among you. What I mean is this, that each one of you [either] says, I belong to Paul, or I belong to Apollos, or I belong to Cephas (Peter), or I belong to Christ.

"The relationships and the health of the relationships in our lives are the guideposts to our destiny fulfillment. In these relationships, discerning motives are critical for each party involved. Having sharp discernment, even with those who desire relationship with you, should be applied according to the purposes of God in your future and assignment.

Conclusion

We are in what could be the finest hour of the Church. It would be very sad to have accomplished everything we desire to accomplish only to be robbed of the opportunity of experiencing the quality of real fellowship with the Lord and others. In our attempts to change the world we must at every level be convicted by the Holy Spirit concerning the offerings of our heart; our dealings with people, and our motives. We must make a commitment to be driven and inspired by one thing, the leading and orchestration of the Lord and a desire to be pleasing to him. Should this be our plea, world change will happen now and around the corner in greater measures. May the spirit of truth continue to draw us away from fraudulent 'Christian' activity into a genuine walk of love, maturity and commitment so that we stop pointless casualties of scandal and reckless behaviors. God strengthen you and your offerings. No MORE STRANGE FIRE!!!!Blessings.

Wow!

Made in the USA
Lexington, KY
21 October 2013